T0120665

THE KEYS TO EFFECTIVE TEACHING

Culturally Revelant Teaching Strategies

DAMEION COWANS SR.

WESTBOW
PRESS®
A DIVISION OF THOMAS NELSON
& ZONDERVAN

WestBow Press books may be ordered through booksellers or by contacting:

WestBow Press
A Division of Thomas Nelson & Zondervan
1663 Liberty Drive
Bloomington, IN 47403
www.westbowpress.com
844-714-3454

ISBN: 978-1-6642-3503-8 (sc)
ISBN: 978-1-6642-3502-1 (hc)
ISBN: 978-1-6642-3504-5 (e)

Library of Congress Control Number: 2021910601

Print information available on the last page.

WestBow Press rev. date: 05/24/2021

CONTENTS

(Student Data Tracker) Behavior, Attendance, Engagement, Assignment Production, PRE-POST DATA

INTRODUCTION

This curriculum was curated to create teaching methods by cultivating ingenuity and dissecting behavior, academic rigor, differentiation, emotional states, and social interaction among colleagues, peers, and students. Stakeholders in education may uniquely manifest self-intrinsic motivation and academic success, and foster positive lifelong mentorship. The C.O.W.A.N.S. (Communication, Ownership, Wins, Analysis, Negativity, Structure) method is a vehicle and indicator that may be used to identify vital elements of a student's psychology, self-awareness, self-perception, and self-motivation, while fostering and highlighting his or her success in urban schools.

FRAMING THE PROBLEM

Generation Z in education are dealing with unique stressors, such as social media, resulting in social anxiety, peer interactions, depression, and lack of belonging. Students now practice alleviating pain and trauma by cutting themselves or, unfortunately, devising suicide plans. The inevitable spectrum of socially acceptable and socially unacceptable behaviors induces psychological fear, which produces stress, trauma, unfocused academics, and negative self-perceptions.

WHAT IS SOCIAL-EMOTIONAL LEARNING (SEL)?

Social-emotional learning is the process in which humans actively engage in positively identifying social and emotional states of being. Social-emotional learning (SEL) is the development of student self-awareness, self-perception, and self-control within the classroom setting. Furthermore, the development of SEL in scholars is essential in careers, homes, and schools.

WHY COWANS SEL?

The COWANS SEL method was curated by an individual who ploughed through the Jefferson County public school system of Birmingham, Alabama, as an at-risk, troubled youth. Early on, his school's standard curriculum curtailed his interest in learning and stunted his academic growth. Unfortunately, while matriculating through schools, this student was suspended, sent to alternative schools, and even expelled. He coped with trauma and everyday stressors, without mentors, role models, or educators as vehicles of guidance and positive transformation. His teachers never promoted social or emotional interactions to entice and cultivate the student's state of being, which could have potentially propelled his engagement, academic success, and self-perception.

While in college, and often disoriented by life, the young man prayed for peace and purpose. This quest for enlightenment led several professors to advise this student that his purpose might be to connect with and help develop students around and across the country. One year later, the student embarked on his journey as an educator. As a first-year teacher, he was recognized as a level-four educator. Pairing passion and risk with his pedagogy allowed him to hone in on each student's health, well-being, learning style, personality, and character, thus leading to the rise of unknowingly practicing and establishing the COWANS SEL curriculum.

The COWANS method was created out of what I hoped for as a student. It is designed for an educator with hope and belief in each student that helps instill permanent change and genuine excitement concerning each student's state of being, academic performance, hope, and career aspirations. Students seek validation from others due to self-perception, self-reflection, and traumas. Meanwhile, educators often tailor students' lives and perceptions.

There are quality educators, great educators, and everlasting educators, but all educators should aspire to be everlasting, creating lifelong memories essential for happiness. All educators should always speak positively over each student, crafting genuine thoughts tailored to each student's weekly emotional state.

Educators should often give verbal praise and be vulnerable. They should genuinely greet each student, and most importantly, be available and prepared for each day. Creating a warm culture as an educator in the classroom is vital. Principals, instructional coaches, deans, and department heads should be vibrant and create friendly cultures within their schools as well.

While doing a casual assessment on states of being, I noticed a student who was weeping. The student stated he did not feel loved or valued, had a negative self-perception, and lacked self-awareness. This led to one of my most memorable class moments. Due to the climate and culture within the classroom that I had created, the entire class embraced the student. This gesture gave rise to one of the many quotes that was used in class: "If no one told you they love you today, remember that Mr. Cowans loves you and always will!"

HOW TO IDENTIFY YOUR SCHOLARS

There are seven identifiable learning styles: auditory, visual, verbal, physical, logical, social, and solitary. Many students are not cognizant of their learning style until junior high or high school. However, teachers can identify each scholar's learning dynamics in how their students' notes are written. Identifying scholars is an essential task that stakeholders of education must develop; identifying learning modalities assists teachers with differentiation and understanding each student's zone proximal development (ZPD).

The first style of learning is auditory. Auditory or aural learners maximize their learning potential through listening and language skills. Aural or auditory learners use responsive speech to increase their learning dynamics.

Many auditory students increase their learning with the use of music or musical tones. Aural learners' career paths can include, but are not limited to, music teachers, speech pathologists, sound engineers, judges, school counselors, and hearing officers.

Spatial or visual learners are often scholars who use maps or diagram concepts. English language learners (ELLs) learn significantly better with the use of visual aids. This assistance alleviates language barriers. Teachers can connect with spatial students via drawings, graphic organizers, or by creating road maps of connections. Careers for these learners can often be, but are not limited to, architecture, art, engineering, interior design, or photography.

Linguistic learners are categorized as scholars who express their learning verbally or in writing. Verbal learners enjoy the mnemonics, are gifted in learning new languages, love study groups, have rich vocabularies, and often have unique ways of verbal expression. As a scholar in the classroom, educators should tailor their methods with the assistance of reading aloud or instructional videos with step-by-step tutorials. Verbal scholars should be tasked with book reports, written assignments, and scripts. Verbal careers can be in journalism, politics, and occupational therapy.

Kinesthetic learners are physical learners or "doers." These scholars are taught using the "I do, we do, you do" method. Kinesthetic learners often learn by touching, moving, or displaying. Kinesthetic learners are well coordinated; many kinesthetic learners share characteristics of attention deficit hyperactivity disorder. Incorporation of story, movement, drawing, or physical expression can stimulate engagement for people with this learning style. Kinesthetic learning careers could be in acting, athletics, art, carpentry, and surgery.

Logical learners appreciate brain functionality and reasoning. These scholars are fond of the complexity of numerical or sequential expressions. They are achievers in mathematics, chemistry, and systematic processes. Scholars identified as logical learners will welcome the Cornell note-taking method. Careers for logical learners can be in accounting, computer science, law, physics, and statistics.

Interpersonal learners are excellent at communicating with and listening to others. Group learning is an effective learning strategy that can propel academic engagement for social learners. Using tools and methods that promote group learning, like small discussion groups and snowball teaching, are often effective. In snowball teaching, scholars toss a ball to others in the class to facilitate discussions. The catcher of the ball contributes to the discussion before tossing the ball to another. Careers for social learners could be in coaching, human resources, politics, sales, and teaching.

Solitary learners are quiet and reserved scholars. These scholars often shelter themselves from others and rarely speak. They analyze, organize, and develop their cognizant states. The intrapersonal student's preference is individualized learning, and they are excellent notetakers. Careers could be in counseling, consulting, psychology, philosophy, and writing.

Teachers can find the most success by differentiating content to ensure each student reaches his or her ZPD. ZPD is the theory that when students receive an assignment, challenge, or task that may be very difficult for them, they can seek help. The task's complexity or level of difficulty should cause the student to seek assistance. Then, with assistance from peers or teachers, the project can be comprehended and completed accurately. Teachers are tasked daily with differentiating and designing content with rigor. Differentiation allows educators to tailor their teaching methods to assist and cover each of these seven learning styles. At the same time, rigor achieves the purposes of meeting each student's ZPD. This daily collaboration of teaching practices promotes engagement, academic success, and comprehension throughout the classroom.

BEHAVIOR

Educators take on a plethora of personalities within their classrooms. While educators have many roles and responsibilities, one key role involves classroom management. Consequently, effective teachers are efficient at behavioral management. Students can be apathetic, annoy others, cheat on assignments, create disruptions, and fight. Teachers must deter this behavior.

Feeling valued can motivate scholars who show apathetic behavior, such as sulking, carelessness, or a lack in motivation. Educators should frequently check in on them and ask specifically about their interests. Always approach each scholar with a warm tone and a smile. Stakeholders who have students always should Be genuine.

Annoying behaviors include name-calling, making jokes at the expense of others, or teasing. It also includes bullying. Educators should frequently circulate the room to give verbal praise to all scholars, thus creating a warm and conducive learning environment. Your environment constitutes your learning; if your environment is poor, student learning will also be poor.

Cheating on assignments often occurs if a student realizes he or she is unable to master an assignment or didn't study for an exam. Consequently, some students may rely on others' assistance in cheating or sneaking notes with the hope of obtaining adequate grades. Thus, cheating can create false narratives in conscientious students.

Educators can alleviate cheating by differentiating content material, thus providing achievements and milestones for those learners. Assist scholars with their ZPDs by assigning the same concepts but expecting different levels of completion due to scholars' developments. Increasing rigor in assignments contributes to each student's development while acknowledging and celebrating success in academics for all students. This promotes growth in those who are approaching grade level as well as those who exemplify mastery. Ultimately, building a foundation of integrity is pertinent. Therefore, educators who increase rigor, differentiate, and celebrate success in all students can successfully alleviate cheating. With all students knowing their individual milestones of academic achievement, rather than all scholars being held to the same mastery level, a culture of integrity is built within the classroom.

Class disruptions may occur frequently. Many cause continuous distractions, laughter, or even embarrassment. Students move, walk, talk, or throw things across the room. Why? Scholars who cause disruptions are disengaged, unaware, or unable to cope with stressors. All disruptions do not warrant a reaction. However, the educator who has a sense of presence can deter disruptions by his or her presence, including being close to the particular student.

Class disruptions or annoyances from others that go mishandled can initiate an altercation. Any educator who perceives unwanted attention to or bullying of others should immediately eliminate this issue. Teachers should address the root of the bullying. Today's students use social media as a lens for conveying their frustrations or thoughts. Therefore, many issues derive from social media accounts. Educators can create social media accounts for themselves to become more relatable to their students. This also allows educators to engage with and disseminate information among parents while monitoring students' social media narratives.

The establishment of classroom norms are essential. Norms assist in tailoring your environment to your scholars. Without norms, students can frequently roam, act maliciously, or become defiant. Norms are mandated as classroom expectations that are principles to alleviate behavior issues or defiant disruptions. As an educator, your classroom norms are vital. However, your classroom culture/environment is paramount. Students will follow your norms *if your norms are consistent and fair.* Teachers should model their norms the first few weeks of school, thereby alleviating any misconceptions. Teaching allows students to use hand signals to signify they want or need something, allowing you to continue to engage while quickly authorizing a scholar to use the restroom, sharpen a pencil, retrieve a tissue, or ask a question. Educators can alleviate the distractions to others while authorizing or answering others' questions. Thus silent signals are vital to maintaining an environment conducive to learning and effectively teaching.

CLIMATE AND PEER INTERACTION

Climate is paramount in any facility or setting. Therefore, positivity within schools is important. Your climate can deter behavior, social anxiety, depression, and suicidal thoughts, and produce a positive, conducive learning environment inside your building. First-year teachers or teachers transferring into a new building must incorporate classroom norms while including culture and climate. For example, if a scholar provides feedback to assist or help other students, teachers should create a positive celebration in the classroom, such as applause or verbal acknowledgment. This propels scholars to assist each other in expectation of verbal praise. As a result, a warm, helpful, family-oriented classroom is created while continuing to uplift culture and celebrate norms and classroom success.

Teachers speak, engage, and develop relationships with all scholars. Educators who foster positive relationships outside academics and support their scholars become prominent figures in their students' lives. Supporting students in clubs, sports, or performances positively affects teacher-student relationships, thus propelling culture. Students of different ethnicities are able to be reached as well and seek out common themes food, culture, and music. During my first year at a diverse school, I was building culture and climate. While I was administering homework and or quizzes, I began asking students to prepare tests and quizzes for me in Spanish and Arabic to increase relationships and also improve my learning in different languages. Students created challenges among different classes to see who could prepare the hardest test for me. Therefore while increasing climate and culture, I created visual data charts to display each class assignment completion percentages, average quiz grades, and average test grades for each month and each class period. While I created my own data charts to display, students created the Mr. Cowans's test and data chart for each week, each class, and each test grade. For example: First block, third block, and sixth block, the October quiz average in Arabic was 42 out of 100, and in Spanish, 85 out of 100. Each class was ecstatic to display my results. Even though my Arabic test grades are failing, the class culture and climate created notions of success, family, and perseverance. Ultimately, the perseverance I displayed in learning new languages from my students correlated to their own level of achievement and discipline in the courses.

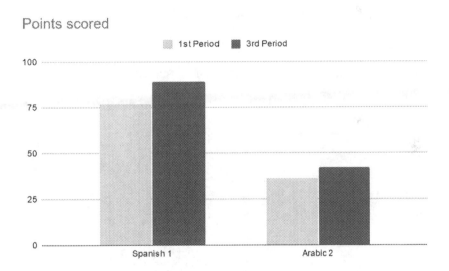

Points scored

■ 1st Period ■ 3rd Period

Educators must adapt their pedagogies to understand each student's personality. Personality can propel or deter friendly interactions and affect peer relationships. When engaging students, examine their ideologies and peer interactions with others. Examination can alleviate negative interactions due to preferential seating, for example. Preferential seating is when a student is placed in a particular seat or area that is conducive to his or her learning environment.

Although scholars interact frequently at school, most negative interactions occur via social platforms. Therefore, as I mentioned previously, educators should create their own social platforms to interact positively with families and students. This tool can disseminate curriculum information and engage with families, while monitoring peer interactions and become privy to student disagreements.

CULTURE-TEACHING SEL TO ELLS AND MINORITIES

Teachers are tasked with disseminating curriculums of learning to their respective students. As states and schools become increasingly diverse, educators are now tasked with tailoring their pedagogies to meet the learning needs of all scholars. Educators must create unique learning opportunities for ELL students. Unique learning propels ELL students' engagement and learning, so innovative learning becomes a vehicle for academic success. The tools used frequently include visuals, collaborative work, scaffolding, and allowing time for processing.

While a language barrier is inevitable with students who recently transitioned to the United States or are unfamiliar with the English language. Teachers' unique learning adaptive styles are paramount. Students may not comprehend your dialect or language. However, visual aids assist with comprehension and drawing inferences. All students need processing time, and ELL students need at least three to five seconds. Processing time allotts for brain recognition or neurons to begin linking sensory cues to the individual. For example, after asking a question, take a short pause for three to five seconds before seeking a response. This provides processing time for in-depth answers. The assistance of images or descriptions creates bridging to content, thus propelling student comprehension and engagement. Collaborative work is also essential to all students yet it promotes dialogues and reflective time in learning to increase in aiding and assisting those who are ELL's students, as it promotes content dialogue, critical thinking, input, and comprehension. Collaborative work allows students or teachers to form groups, disseminate information, apply theories, and gain feedback from peers. This engagement practice allows ELL students to comprehend content knowledge and concepts more completely while hearing academic language.

Scaffolding is the vehicle for rigorous design content. Scaffolding is the avenue that bridges student learning and comprehension. It occurs through students' learning difficulties and progression to mastery. Educators disseminate content while student comprehension or content knowledge is tested.

Scaffolding shows difficulties in comprehension or knowledge experienced by the student who is unable to produce thorough understanding. Thus, assistance is needed. Differentiation begins, in which one group of students receives assistance and another group continues with critical thinking and posing questions. Another group designs concepts. Each level is strengthening and elevating their knowledge of the content.

Processing times are vital. As mentioned previously, students' time is approximately three to five seconds. This allows neuron triggers, or communication, to signal their brains and elicit a response. Processing time allows students to create exemplary responses. Call and response methods should also be "popcorn," which invokes other scholars to produce quality in-depth answers. The popcorn method assists all scholars in the room to comprehend the content more completely thus maximizes learning. When posing questions, educators should pose high level or complex questions then begin to disseminate the question in order for all students to comprehend.

STUDENT ENGAGEMENT

Student engagement is paramount and the importance of it as it relates to classroom learning. Scholars are expected to be taught daily and to become adept in classroom content. Students are tasked with staying engaged, but the attention span of an adolescent is limited. While educators are tasked with learning and understanding the complexity of student-learning dynamics, many attempt to deliver instruction in a traditional manner. Ultimately, the traditional method delivers boredom, lowers, and limits the learning of today's scholars.

Avenues to increase students' learning include: partner collaborating, peer questioning and peer-strengthening answer statements, technology aids, and incorporating movement. Students become disengaged due to routines or traditional teaching. Students are excited to receive praise from their peers or educators. Thus, for several students, answering a question increases rigor and depth while other scholars provide vital feedback. Another questioning skill to incorporate is to allow students who exhibit mastery on the content to create quiz or test questions. This promotes engagement and academic learning. It also increases student participation and willingness to achieve mastery.

STUDENT INTRINSIC MOTIVATION

Student intrinsic motivation is the self-perception of oneself. Motivating yourself or your students' can become complicated, tiresome, and even inadequate. Students may wonder, *How can I become motivated if my reflection or lifestyle is different from my present state?* A student's self-intrinsic motivation starts with a vision of his or her future outcomes and goals. Consistently verbalize goals, dreams, ambitions, self-perception, self-worth, and self-values. Dream as if you've already earned it; think as if you've already obtained it. The fruition of your goals, self-worth, and self-value arrive through consistently verbalizing your outcomes and seeking the vehicle of change as it simultaneously manifests in yourself. Believing that you can accomplish your goals and dreams aids your self-motivation.

As educators, motivate students daily. Create differentiated assignments that allow students to exhibit their strengths. If an educator creates a presentation assignment, allow students to incorporate artistic, technological, or verbal creativity skills. After primary school, many students' creativity becomes boxed in or lessens due to specific ramifications. Students' creative motivations or engagements also decline.

Veteran educators are keen on their students' learning dynamics. In each class, give verbal praise and compliment your students while setting a standard of high expectations and cognitive development among them. Students have many external stressors, and their place of peace is often your classroom. As an educator, you're tasked to be a secondary guardian. Develop an outgoing, approachable personality. Become intrigued by their interests. Supporting students in their extracurricular activities gives students the perception that you care about them as individuals as well as students. Adolescents often simply wish to know you care or that they matter. The mindset of caring or displaying positive understanding of their circumstances or environments fosters an essential bond that goes far beyond the classroom.

Students frequently need guidance in propelling their self-intrinsic values. Self-esteem issues frequently plague adolescents. The increased use of social media has created the notion that a video or a single picture is an individual's reality. However, it creates a psychological false perception of those individuals' lives. This is an issue that creates depression and negative self-perception, which becomes a bridge for negative self-intrinsic value.

DIFFERENTIATION

Differentiation is the art of skillfully and consistently balancing content delivery to assist scholars by providing effective methods that adapt to each student's ZPD. A state's end-of-year assessment has become increasingly important in education. Teachers are evaluated by their students' scoring on the state's assessment, correlating with teachers' evaluation scores. The lens of effective differentiation begins with understanding each student's academic progress within the given standard. For example: A student in the seventh grade will be examined in his or her Life Science course on chapter one section one. (7. Life Science (LS) 1.1) Scholar A exhibited below proficient, Scholar B exhibited mastery, and Scholar C exhibited on grade level. While understanding their progress through assignments, in-class response, quizzes, and tests, each content delivery is devoted to increasing comprehension by alleviating students' standard lapses.

Within given standards, the trajectory of the example above for Scholar A, depending on his or her learning modalities, needs content delivery through the use of visual or audio means, or peer-strengthening feedback. Scholar B can assist with high-level questioning while tailoring his or her responses to three-dimensional answers. Differentiation must continue to increase the excellence of academic learning within the given standard for the scholar who exhibited mastery. Scholar C has exhibited on grade level. These scholars are often overlooked due to students who are either approaching or are above grade-level mastery. However, this could be the majority of your scholars and require you to push and strengthen your differentiation skills. Differentiation requires proper planning to assist students.

Student's Name	Learning Modality	Differentiation Preference	Below Grade Level On Grade Level Mastery

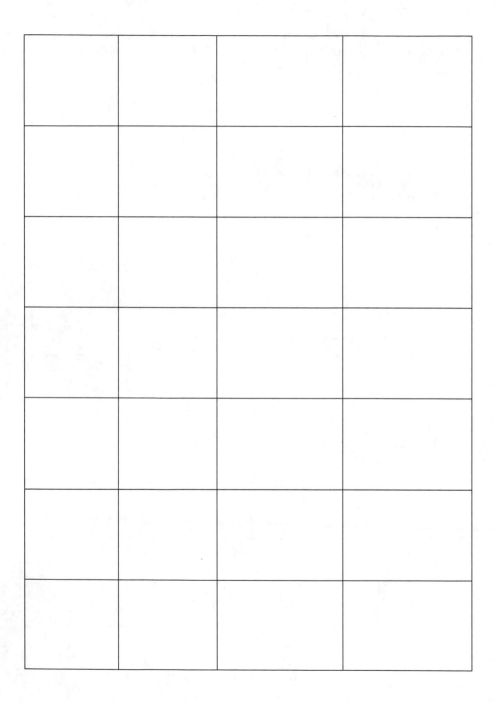

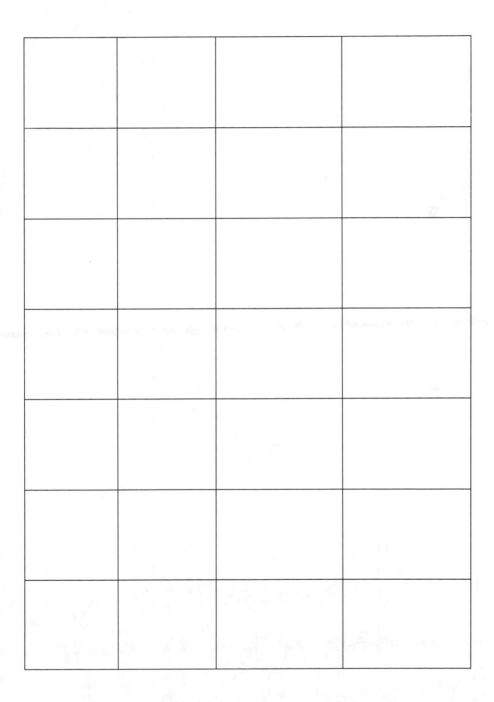

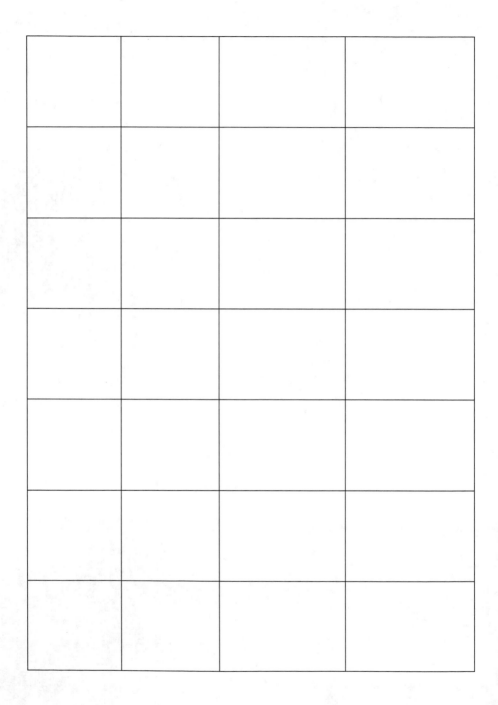

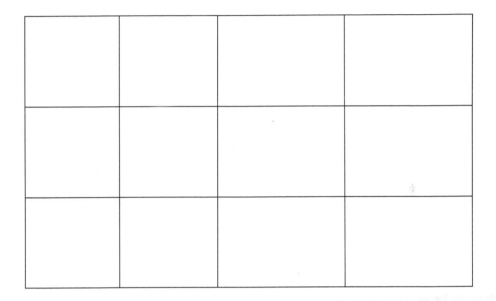

TEACHING THE COWANS METHOD

COWANS SEL Curriculum

Key Components

- Have a good attitude. Teachers should be approachable and open.
- Create an environment that is welcoming and conducive to learning.
- Build positive relationships while exuding confidence.

- Pose questions to students daily or weekly regarding social health and well-being.
- Deliver content enthusiastically and engagingly, thereby creating a productive atmosphere.

Understanding the COWANS Method

C—Communication. Frequently communicate with your students regarding their life issues, nothing content-based.

O—Ownership. After communicating, allow students to choose ownership of life and actions.

W—Wins. Publicly celebrate every win, even the small ones.

A—Analysis. All student interactions are important. Analyze each student's social, emotional, and behavioral interactions.

N—Negativity. Eliminate negative interactions. Assist students in replacing those with positive thoughts.

S—Structure. While performing the COWANS method, ensure that students remain or become structured to deter negative behaviors while promoting academic successes.

SAMPLE LESSON

Tailoring SEL while Teaching
Forty-Five-Minute Courses

10:05 a.m.—Bell ringers are projected / student check-in demonstration throughout the class.

10:05–10:10 a.m.—Flow of class is important, emphasize procedures and consistency.

10:10–10:20 a.m.—Promote positive energy, recognize those who are working, students' have a unique personality and speak, yet allow them to be engaged in the material.

10:20–10:35 a.m.—Deliver content, create turn-and-talk, allow students to create high-level questioning to pair with shoulder partners, and create the parent call-home list.

10:40 a.m.—Place positive calls to students' homes, which allows parents to know the positive aspects of their children's academics. Why?

10:45 a.m.—Share a small yet influential quote about winning with students. Simple is effective.

10:50–11:00 a.m.—Teachers should use data to transform the classroom and those who increase or show proficiency are awarded jobs within the classroom. Create class jobs that rotate weekly.

For example, teachers should create a grid list of letters that correspond to each class (A- first period, B- Second Period, C-Third Period, D- Fourth Period, and etc. The number of students within the class. Create a master list to identify each student. Use of a moving grid as a lens of mastery for students in each section or unit. The Grid list could illustrate A 13- which corresponds to a student in the first block who is selected to become number 13 in this course. The metrics I use are the following: testing, homework, class participation, and attendance.

EFFECTIVE VIRTUAL TEACHING

Unprecedented times during COVID-19 have altered our traditional format of educating our students. Nevertheless, content delivery is essential and paramount. Scholars are expected to continue learning on virtual platforms or flipped-classroom models. To teach effectively during COVID-19, teachers must adapt to the new norm. First, understanding your student audience is important. Educators should complete their analyses of learning complexities that propel student engagement. Students will be tasked with strengthening their understanding. Teachers should pose questions every three minutes for response, critical thinking, and to elucidate explanations. Teachers should not teach more than five consecutive minutes. Teaching several consecutive minutes without student engagement will lead to boredom, unenthusiastic students, and lack of learning.

Flipped classrooms allow educators to present the content and pose questions to students. Once finished, teachers and students engage in dialogue regarding content to clarify or ensure mastery of standards and subject concepts.

Virtual platforms have become an essential classroom during our new norm of education. These platforms have afforded us the opportunity to continue educating scholars while effectively tailoring our pedagogy to ensure learning remains at the forefront of education.

PRINCIPALS' CORNER

Principals' corner is designed to become an avenue to assist principals by increasing their staff's level of effectiveness and evaluation scores. Educators are tasked with a plethora of assignments as teachers. However, routine follow-ups to ensure your staff is mentally and emotionally well are vital. Therefore, creating a biweekly check-in list promotes morale, creates a warm culture, and fosters the notion of principal support within each teacher.

Principals' corner is curated to produce dialogue regarding scholastic achievement and to highlight educators who are model teachers for their schools. Highlighting educators fosters teacher retention and offsets negative perceptions while creating a conducive learning culture. Effectively following up with staff to gauge perception, emotional well-being, academic rigor, or behavioral expectations is a bridge for teacher retention and satisfaction within your school.

Biweekly check-ins can range from informal dialogues to scheduling conferences. This method provides principals a lens, a foundation of cultures, behaviors, and academics within their school, while teachers' perceptions of their schools are parallel with students' progress and behavior in their courses.

Visionary Student's Manual
(Social Emotional Learning)

COWANS'
CONSULTING

WHAT IS SOCIAL-EMOTIONAL LEARNING (SEL)?

Social-emotional learning (SEL) is the process by which humans actively engage in positively identifying the social and emotional states of being. SEL is the development of student self-awareness, self-perception, and self-control. Furthermore, the development of SEL in scholars is essential in careers, homes, and schools. SEL is a vehicle to students' self-intrinsic value or self-perception.

Teachers and family members can often propel students' defined values of themselves. The influence of social platforms has negatively affected many adolescents. Social media displays one's highlights in life. In contrast, others correlate stress with their reality, which creates stressors or negative perceptions of their existence.

STUDENT INTRINSIC MOTIVATION

Student intrinsic motivation is the self-perception of oneself. Motivating yourself can be complicated, tiresome, and even inadequate. Students may wonder, *How can I become motivated if my reflection or lifestyle is different from my present state?*

Students' self-intrinsic motivation starts with a vision of one's future outcomes and goals. Consistently verbalize goals, dreams, ambitions, self-perceptions, self-worth, and self-values. Dream as if you've already earned it; think as if you've already obtained it. The fruition of your goals, self-worth, and self-value arrives through consistently verbalizing your outcomes and seeking the vehicle of change as it simultaneously manifests in you. Believe that you can accomplish your goals and dreams, and self-motivate.

MY LIFE

"My Life" is created to seek particular times in your life in writing. It allows you to reflect on specific times in your life while envisioning future outcomes. To assist in writing, here are some moments you can write about: parents and significant people during your upbringing, joys, experiences, school, family traditions, house chores or duties, sports, religion, your highlights, and profound skills in life, and so on. My example follows.

My Life

I arrived into the world on October 31. I was born in Birmingham, Alabama. I was born in a single-parent household. I was expelled from daycare. I was sent to alternative school several times. I graduated from college and graduate school. My upbringing does not define me, yet it propelled me to achieve greatness.

This "My Life" isn't typical, but it is mine. On the following page you will have the opportunity to write out your life story. "My Life" is an avenue to your experiences along with future ambitions. It is designed to highlight past trauma while becoming conscious of your destiny-intended future. This method allows therapeutic writing, thus creating awareness of one's profound self.

VISION

Your vision is the vehicle to your future outcome.

The ability to imagine your future success and outcome is precedent. Vision aligning with goals becomes attainable through progress. In this section, write and explain how you can attain your one-month to one-year vision.

One Month

_____

_____

_____

_____

_____

_____

_____

_____

Six Months

_____

_____

_____

_____

_____

_____

_____

One Year

_____

_____

_____

_____

_____

_____

_____

Are your visions and goals consistent with your actions?

_____

_____

_____

_____

_____

_____

_____

How can you ensure you obtain your goals without disruptions?

_____

_____

_____

_____

_____

_____

_____

IDENTIFYING YOURSELF

What are your values?

_____

_____

_____

_____

_____

_____

_____

_____

In which way do you learn: visual, kinesthetic, or auditory?

_____

_____

_____

_____

_____

_____

_____

_____

How do you define yourself?

_____

_____

_____

_____

_____

SEL CALENDAR

Sun	Mon	Tue	Wed	Thu	Fri	Sat
	What is SEL?	How has trauma affected me?	How can I overcome trauma?	What does a stressor look like?	Social versus reality	

	Family's expectation versus reality	What is my impact on others?	How am I affected by others?	Do outside interactions create my thoughts?	How can I motivate others?	
	How are my actions perceived by others?	Are my actions altered once I leave home?	Am I true to myself? Esse quam videri.	Does social media negatively affect my life?	Am I motivated by myself?	

	Speaking positively	Eliminating others' opinions	Improving self-value	Exceeding expected potential	Promoting and living the new you	
	Exuding positive energy	Renewing your mind				

REMIND ME 10:10

Remind Me 10:10 allows students to write down any essential tasks to be completed. This should be used frequently.

_____

_____

_____

_____

_____

_____

_____

_____

_____

_____

_____

_____

_____

MY JOURNAL AND THOUGHTS

_____

_____

_____

_____

_____

_____

_____

_____

_____

_____

_____

_____

_____

_____

_____

_____

_____

_____

_____

_____

_____

_____

_____

_____

_____

_____

_____

_____

_____

_____

_____

_____

_____

_____

_____

_____

_____

_____

GLOSSARY

Auditory- Students who have the ability by hearing and processing information.

Curriculum- a set of lessons or activities designed to enhance educational learning.

Dissemination- The process of passing information from teacher to students in a wide variety of contexts.

Differentiation- The process of teaching multiple learning styles to aid in student learning.

English Language Learners "ELL"- students who are learning the English language.

Stakeholders- Constituents who are prominent members in students' education (family, teachers, and community partners).

Interpersonal- Students who effectively communicate with other students to increase learning and academic dialogue.

Linguistic- Students who learn in writing.

Logical- Students who learn by complexity of numbers.

Kinesthetic- Students who learn and process information by moving

Spatial or Visual- students who learn by seeing information or content in real time.

Social Emotional Learning- the task of incorporating positive relationships and affirmation to students or colleagues. Assisting in managing emotions to build positive future outcomes.

Zone Proximal Development- Student ability to process information at the highest level without needing assistance in clarifying content work or problems.

STUDENTS LEARNING ASSESSMENT

1. **What type of book would you like to read?**

   A. A book with a lot of words

   B. A book with pictures

   C. A book that is read to me

   D. A book that you would read to incorporate movements.

2. **You are researching a science project, are you more likely to?**

   A. Watch a video on the project sequencing

   B. Read an article about the project

   C. You will listen to audio regarding projects

   D. You will learn more about the project by conducting steps yourself.

3. **If someone is purchasing a pair of shoes in line, while waiting to checkout, what would you do?**
   A. See the shoes physically
   B. Prefer to listen how they are in detail
   C. Not ask

4. **When learning how to play a new card game would you?**
   A. Learn from friends
   B. Listen to their explanations
   C. Read the instructions
   D. Learn from others by watching the game.

5. **Your family is going on a vacation would you like to?**
   A. Read the itinerary
   B. Use a map to view attractions in the city you are visiting
   C. Talk with your family about who planned the trip
   D. Look at the details and highlight possible attractions

6. **What is the best way for you to study?**

    A. Have a friend quiz you

    B. Write out questions and answers on index cards

    C. Review your notes on using pictures or graphs

    D. Quiet place of study and focus

7. If you were to build a desk you bought on the internet would you

    A. Would you look at the box and begin building

    B. Read the instructions

    C. Watch a video on building the desk

    D. Listen to someone who can teach you how to build the desk

8. Your school had a school dance, what would you remember most about the dance?

    A. The music was played

    B. Who all you saw at the dance

    C. The environment of the dance

    D. The dances you did at the dance

9. What is your favorite class
    A. Math Class
    B. Gym Class
    C. Art Class

10. When you hear a new song
    A. Start dancing or doing rhythmic moves
    B. Picture a video production that goes along with the song
    C. Research the lyrics
    D. Replay the song over and over

11. What is your favorite way to relax
    A. Listen to music
    B. Watch videos
    C. Read
    D. Exercise

12. What distract you the most in class
    A. Students walking pass the classroom
    B. Maintenance cutting the school's grass
    C. The classroom temperature is hot or cold

13. Which of the following would be your favorite prize you won at the fair?

    A. A poster

    B. A sports ball (Basketball, football, or soccer)

    C. A new music album

14. What would you rather do with friends?

    A. Go to a concert

    B. Go to the Movies

    C. Go to an amusement park

15. I prefer a teacher who uses

    A. Visual diagrams

    B. Books

    C. Demonstration

EXPLANATION FOR SELECTED LEARNING STYLES

Learning styles are complex, yet this is a motivational strategy for all learning to know how or ways to incorporate or build their learning. If you (the student) prefer to learn by listening the student is an auditory learner. If the student learns by visual aids the student is a visual learner. If the student learns by the use of complex numbering or language, the student will be a logical learner. If the student learns with the incorporation of movement the student is a kinesthetic learner.

Students may be deemed as more than one learning style. Students are unique therefore do not limit the classification of learning styles tailor each teaching moment to bridge the learning to the complexity in assisting all styles therefore this will be incorporating student learning differentiation.

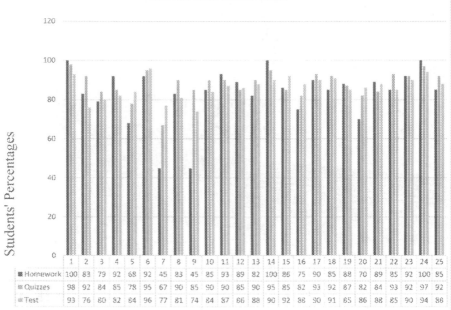

Student Data Tracker Chart

	1	2	3	4	5	6	7	8	9	10	11	12	13	14	15	16	17	18	19	20	21	22	23	24	25
Homework	100	83	79	92	68	92	45	83	45	85	93	89	82	100	86	75	90	85	88	70	89	85	92	100	85
Quizzes	98	92	84	85	78	95	67	90	85	90	90	85	90	95	85	82	93	92	87	82	84	93	92	97	92
Test	93	76	80	82	84	96	77	81	74	84	87	86	88	90	92	88	90	91	85	86	88	85	90	94	88

■ Homework   ■ Quizzes   ■ Test

Student Data Chart Tracker